Order in the Body

ADVICE FOR THE
SINGLE AND MARRIED

WOMEN of ORDER

I0082123

SHIELA M. KEAISE   &   MAGDLINE MONROE

MARTINA
PUBLISHING
INC.

Walterboro, South Carolina

Library of Congress Control Number: 2017903097

Order in the Body: Advice for the Single and Married/Shiela M. Keaise and Magdline Monroe. Summary: These Christian authors offer insight into how a woman's life can have order in the body by sharing perspectives in being single versus being married.

Scripture quotations from:
The Holy Bible, King James Version. © 2015 All Rights Reserved.

Martina Publishing, Inc.
PO Box 1216, Walterboro, SC 29488
www.ShielaMartina.com

ISBN-13: 978-0-9799344-4-5

[1. Women—Single/Married. 2. Parts of the Body—Christian Living. 3. Godly Lifestyle—Nonfiction. 4. Bible—King James Version.] I. Title.

Printed in the United States of America

Dedication

SK

This book is dedicated to men and women who want to know their purposes and want to fulfill them through their bodies with God's help.

MM

This book is dedicated to my family God has blessed me with: My husband, Mark and our children, Solomon, David, Tabitha, Jonathan, Jeremiah, Bethany, and Timothy Monroe. My prayer is that God will continue to order our steps according to His perfect will for our lives.

Contents

INTRODUCTION 5

CONCLUSION 54

Introduction

As a 20 year veteran children's librarian in a public library, I enjoy the company of children and observing their behavior. Observing children well is what makes my job interesting and effective. While observing these children, it is obvious how they are governed at home. The child that obeys and responds with respect is the child who is under order in the home. Order is necessary if chaos is not wanted. Chaos is simply defined as behavior so unpredictable as to appear random. Since God is unchanging and very predictable, chaos is not what we want. Although there are a number of excellent books available on being single and/or married, God lead me to Magdline Monroe to write about being women of order, from both the single and married viewpoint with a Godly perspective.

When I called Mrs. Monroe with what God spoke to me about what to write, Mrs. Monroe revealed that God spoke to her about writing about the married life. I told Mrs. Monroe that God wants us to be examples of women of order. She gladly accepted the call and we have worked on this book for 5 years. As we share our experiences, we also want to share the importance of honoring God with our bodies. Not only are we Christian women, we are professional educators with a Godly resolve. The Bible is our main source, because it is the law of God that helps us to put order in the body or maintain that order. As we wrote on the single and married perspective, we wanted to end each section with a song and a prayer. Hopefully, as you read the book, you will sing and pray your way into the proper order in your body. Our goal in writing this book is to share the importance of bringing our body in subjection to how God wants us to live. After reading this book, our prayer is that you will express order in your body and keep this song on your mind as you allow the Lord to bring order to your body as we, too, endeavor to do on a daily basis—***Oh, Be Careful... Little Eyes, Feet, Mind, Ears, Tongue, Heart, and Hands What You Do.*** May you find peace, love, and a productive life as you allow God to order your steps.

Order Your
WEIGHT

· · · · · · · · · · · · · · · · · ·

Matthew 6:25
Therefore I tell you, do not be anxious about your life, what you
will eat or what you will drink, nor about your body, what you will
put on. Is not life more than food, and the body more than
clothing?

If we are to be successful in keeping our weight under control, we must first have a desire to be healthy. We should take control of our body image for self-respect's sake. That is why it is important for women to not let our weight control us, instead we control our weight. Ultimately, men look at women, not because they are fat or thin, but because they are confident and have respect for themselves. Granted some frames are bigger or smaller than others; however, as long as that frame is healthy, happy and in the will of God, there is no reason for wanting someone else's frame or changing it to suit someone else.

We know that God has given each of us a special frame. Although we single women care if men like the way we look, this does not mean we have to base our physical appearance on what men think about our weight. Weight carries a lot of baggage and can be a hindrance to all those who are controlled by it. Basing our weight desire on being pleasing to a man's eye is not worth the effort. Being healthy should be the ultimate deciding factor in the single person's weight goal.

One thing I have learned over the years is that each woman has control over her destiny, whether it is one's lifestyle or one's weight. Philippians 4:13 says, "I can do all things through Christ who strengthens me." For me, being thin was part genetic and part choice… as I always ate little, limited my high calorie intake, and kept myself active most of the time. Although my desire for food was not as great as others, I still had the opportunity to splurge, sit, and do nothing. With food always cooked and ready to serve, it was easy for me to just sit back, eat good food all day, and care less about staying active. Instead of just giving in to laziness, I chose to help out cooking, eat an average portion and stay dutiful at home, at church, on my job, and in the community.

Although most smart singles stay busy helping as needed, wherever necessary, there are some truth factors that each of us must confess. First and foremost, do we stop eating when we are satisfied or full? Do we eat more than two pieces of something that is absolutely delicious to our taste buds? Do we sneak high calorie snacks late at night? Do we feel comfortable eating larger portions rather than smaller or medium ones? If we honestly answer these questions and make wise decisions to do the right thing, we are well on our way to gaining control of and maintaining our weight. Then, we can say with a surety that I have ordered my weight with the help of the Lord.

A Song to Sing:
I Want to Live So God Can Use Me

Verse 1:
I'm gonna live so God can use me
Anywhere, Lord, anytime.
I'm gonna live so God can use me
Anywhere, Lord, anytime.

Verse 2:
I'm gonna work so God can use me...

Verse 3:
I'm gonna pray so God can use me...

Verse 4:
I'm gonna sing so God can use me...

Verse 5:
I'm gonna dress so God can use me...

Verse 6:
I'm gonna eat so God can use me...

Verse 7:
I'm gonna love so God can use me...

Verse 8:
I'm gonna live so God can use me
Anywhere, Lord, anytime.
I'm gonna live so God can use me
Anywhere, Lord, anytime.

• • •

Order Your
WEIGHT

· · · · · · · · · · · · · · · · · · · ·

Hebrew 12:1
...let us lay aside every weight, and the sin which doth so easily beset us....

Women come in different shapes and sizes. When in the prime of our lives, some are said to have the shape of a figure eight. However, as some women grow older and get families of their own, those figure eights sometimes extend into figure zeros. Likewise, some men loose their six packs along the way. These shape changes are sometimes a result of eating too much and exercising too little. According to the Word, too much of anything is sin. Therefore, it is not good for us to sit down and over indulge in our favorite foods. As some say, "Everything that is good to you...may not be good for you."

It is easy for some to get so involved in the daily activities of their families that they forget to take time for self. Rather than taking time to go to the gym, we busy ourselves making sure our children are at the gym on time for practice. Rather than taking time to plan and prepare healthy meals, we find ourselves conveniently going through the drive-thru of a fast-food restaurant. These two actions alone will cause one to put on unwanted weight.

As we strive to be good caretakers of our families, if we are not careful, we can very easily neglect to take care of ourselves. I have heard that charity starts at home. People with families need to realize before we can take good care of our families, we must first take good care of ourselves.

A good starting point for us to take care of ourselves is to focus on maintaining a weight that makes us look good and feel good. Usually, we gain weight as a result of what is put on...but is not taken off. We can strive for a healthy weight by monitoring our portions, making healthy food choices, and exercising regularly.

For individuals with families, this can be done by joining in on some family activities. We can take a walk with our spouse and/ or the family; go for a bike ride; or even play a game of softball, basketball, kickball, etc.

When focusing on an ideal weight, it is not as much as what others think...but what you think about yourself that counts most. Since obesity leads to many health issues, it would be to our advantage to maintain an idea weight that makes us look good and feel good. However, regardless of what our weight is, we must not allow ourselves to become overly consumed with trying to be a certain size. We should not let our weight burden us down, because God loves us regardless of what size we are. Therefore, we should love ourselves. We should not allow our weight or the weights (or issues) of our marriage or life to discourage us.

A Prayer to Pray:

Heavenly Father,
Help me to order my life according to Your perfect will. Help me
to take good care of this body you have blessed me with. Guide
me in my decisions as to what to feed my body that I may nourish
and strengthen it. Everything that would bring harm to my body
or weigh me down in life, I bound in the name of Jesus. I loose
those good things to strengthen and nourish not only my body,
but my spouse, my marriage, and my family.
In Jesus' name I pray. Amen.

• • • •

Order Your EYES

. . . .

Psalms 119:37
Turn away mine eyes from beholding vanity and quicken thou me
in thy way.

Luke 11:34
The light of the body is the eye: therefore when thine eye is single,
thy whole body also is full of light; but when thine eye is evil, thy
body also is full of darkness.

It is a true saying that "Beauty is in the eyes of the beholder."
Yet no one has ever considered that, "It depends on whose eyes
are looking." In other words, everyone sees things her own way.
While the natural eye captures the essence of what is visible, it
takes a spiritual eye to see beyond the natural. I was taught that
you can't watch everything or anything and easily observe
spiritual things. My television time was limited as a child. I was
only allowed 2 hours a day to watch certain shows. This made a
difference in how I disciplined myself in situations and operated
on a day-to-day basis.

The Bible says, "Turn away your eyes from beholding vanity." This tells me that we should not look at things that are of no value. Things that look really good and seem the most desirable are the very things that can lead us astray from the truth. Consequently, whatever we watch on a regular basis will influence our thinking, and ultimately our behavior.

The Bible tells us when the eye is single or focused, the whole body is full of light; but when the eye is evil, the body is filled with darkness. Once the light fills our body, we can lighten the darkened world. We ought to let our light so shine before men, that they may see our good works, and glorify our Father which is in heaven (Matthew 5:16). Giving a good perception of what is good and true often comes to light. That is why it is important to have spiritual eyes to see as God sees.

You see, light is truth and darkness is sin. A sure way to please God is to allow the light of God's Word to fill our eyes. Once our eyes behold truth, we can order our body to spread the light everywhere we go. If we want to walk in truth, we must accept God's Holy Word; so we will be able to spread God's light. By using our eyes to see the truth in God's Word, in our sisters and brothers, and in our situation, we are allowing the light to fill our bodies.

Not only does Proverbs 20:13 advises us to "love not sleep, lest we come to poverty," it also advises us to "open our eyes and we shall be satisfied with bread." This tells us as single women to get a sufficient amount of sleep, but we should not overdo it by sleeping too much when we could be working. Ordering our eyes means seeing the natural, spiritual, and physical needs and being dutiful enough to work out our soul's salvation. When our eyes are ordered by God, it will truly do good to the entire body!

A Song to Sing:
This Little Light of Mine

Verse 1:
This little light of mine (caller)
I'm going to let it shine (response)
Oh, this little light of mine (caller)
I'm going to let it shine (response)
Hallelujah (all)
This little light of mine (caller)
I'm going to let it shine (response)
Let it shine, let it shine, let it shine (all)

Verse 2:
Everywhere I go (caller)
I'm going to let it shine (response)...

Verse 3:
All in my house (caller)
I'm going to let it shine (response)...

Verse 4:
All on my job (caller)
I'm going to let it shine (response)...

Verse 5:
Out on the byways (caller)
I'm going to let it shine (response)...

(You may add wherever you desire to let your light shine)

• • •

Order Your
EYES

. . . .

Genesis 13: 14-15
And the Lord said unto Abram after that Lot was separated from him, Lift up now thine eyes, and look from the place where thou art…: For all the land which thou seest, to thee will I give it, and to thy seed forever.

Our eyes are our mechanism for seeing the world around us. Some say beauty is in the eyes of the beholder. To me, this means that we all see things differently. Two individuals can look upon the exact same item, and yet have different perspectives concerning the item. One may see the glass half full, while the other may see the glass half empty. However you see things will determine your approach in dealing with things. If you perceive or see that you have a chance of accomplishing your goals, there's a good chance that you will pursue your goals. However, if through your perception, you don't see too much of a chance of success, chances are…you won't pursue what you view as potential failure.

Some say…*with God the sky is the limit.* I believe…*with God there is no limit!* When Abraham and Lot came to the point of separation in the book of Genesis, God told Abraham to look out over the land. As far as Abraham could see, God said He would give it unto Abraham. So it is with us today. What we can see and trust God for, God will give it unto us. So I ask...what do you see God doing for you? Can you see God opening closed doors for you? Can you see God closing doors that no longer need to be open in your life? Do you see God meeting you at your point of need?

In life, we will face many challenges. Our spouse, our children, or even the family pet may not always respond the way we would like for them to. Family finances may get scarce...and don't mention when transportation is scarce.... When things go contrary to our liking, we should not get discouraged. Instead, we should look and see the opportunities God has to turn things around in our lives. When we are weak, we must see God as the strong tower in our lives.

I ask the question...how good is your vision? What do you see? Do you see opposition in your life or do you see opportunity? Let me remind you...if God be for you, it is better than the whole world against you. Man's opposition is simply an opportunity for God to perform great and mighty miracles in your life. As far as you can see, God will perform and give it unto you. As Rafiki told Simba (in the movie The Lion King) to look deeper, so I say to you also. Look deeper. Look beyond self (and the challenges and lack in your life, even in your marriage) and look to Calvary's Hill where Jesus died on the cross but rose with all power in His hand. So rather than focusing on your shortcoming, focus on Jesus' strength and trust Him to work everything to your good. I have heard it said that a picture is worth a thousand words....

Well, see and picture things as you would have them in your life as well as in your marriage… and trust the Lord to bring it to past.

A Prayer to Pray:

Heavenly Father,
Order my eyes that I may see the good in my spouse, my marriage,
and my family. Help me to look beyond the obstacles that come
our way...and look unto you the author and finisher of my faith.
Open my eyes that I might see the good things that you have in
store for us. In Jesus' name I pray. Amen.

• • • •

Order Your **EARS**

. . . .

John 5:25
Verily, verily, I say unto you, "The hour is coming, and now is, when the dead shall hear the voice of the Son of God: and they that hear shall live."

As single men and women, it is essential that we be careful to listen to what God has ordained for our lives. We must listen to the places God wants us to go, the things God wants us to do, and the words God wants us to say. It should be our daily desire and mission to be pleasing in God's sight. Thus, it is important to note that obtaining a listening ear is acquired by practice.

Many people fail to realize the significance of listening to wise council. Growing up, we gain this experience by being alert to what our parents instruct us. Not only should we listen to wise instructions in the home, it behooves us to obey them. If we listen to our parents or those who have rule over us while we are young, we start the process of obeying God and other superiors in the workplace, in the church, in the community, and ultimately abroad. No doubt, listening and obeying starts in the home and spreads abroad. By opening our ears to truth, we hear what we need to function, grow, and develop into single Christian women.

The Bible instructs that if we adhere to Jesus' words, we will live. Additionally, as we continue to listen to God's Word, we build our faith. Being taken to Sunday School as a child and now attending weekly Bible Study as an adult have helped me to maintain my Christian faith. Any way you look at it, God promised to bless us when we listen and obey.

What I know for sure is that when we listen to negative speech and/or music, we will condone contrary attitudes and accept dangerous behavior. That is why single people should monitor what we listen to, because everything we listen to goes into our spirit and influences our behavior for good or evil. Thus, we have a choice whether we will live in peace or torment. By ordering our ears to hear and obey the truth, we will choose to live peaceful, contented lives.

A Song to Sing:
Will You Be Ready To Answer The Call

Will you be ready to answer the call
Have you been faithful to Jesus at all
If an angel were to call you into judgement right now,
will you be ready to answer the call.

• • •

Order Your
EARS

. . . .

Romans 10:17
So then faith cometh by hearing, and hearing by the word of God.

With our ears we listen to the different sounds and conversations that surround us. As a mother, I have always advised my children not to listen to any and everything. What you listen to with your ears can easily become deeply embedded within your heart. Some say…what's in you will come out.

I believe the more you listen to something, the more it will take root within you. It's like practicing. We practice to become good at or perfect whatever we practice. Usually, the more we practice, the better we get.

So it is with the things we listen to with our ears. The more we hear it, the more familiar it is to us. Experience has taught me that whether I want something to be a part of me or not, if I listen to it long enough…it will be in me. I was surprised when I realized I was singing the words of a song that I was not familiar with. I finally realized that I had been listening to the radio passively; but at the same time, the words of the songs were being stored within me. Therefore, as the song began to play, the words just spontaneously came forth.

According to the word, faith comes by hearing and hearing by the word of God. This scripture shows that what enters our ears has a direct influence on us as individuals. If you want to build your faith, keep listening to the word of God. Listen to music that inspires you in your faith walk. Whether it seems like anything is happening or not, just keep listening and know that the seed is being planted within. When you need it most, God will bring it to your remembrance.

On the other hand, if you fill your ears with negative words... when under the right pressure, they too will surface.

We must choose wisely as to what we allow to enter our ears. Our ears are like a gateway to the heart. What we let on the inside...can eventually work its way back to the outside through our speech and our actions.

Likewise, if you want to build or strengthen your marriage, speak loving and encouraging words to your spouse. Whether it seems like it or not, your spouse is listening to what you are saying.

A Prayer to Pray:

Heavenly Father,
As You speak, open my ears that I may hear You clearly. As I hear
Your voice, help me to obey. Not only that Lord, but help me to
listen attentively to what my spouse is saying to me. Help us to
not just listen to the words that come out, but with tender loving
care try to sincerely hear what each other is saying. In Jesus' name
I pray. Amen.

• • • •

Order Your TONGUE

. . . .

Proverbs 18:21
Death and life are in the power of the tongue: and they that love it
shall eat the fruit thereof.

Throughout American history and the history of human kind, the tongue has been a powerful tool in bringing about change. It was not mere rhetoric that lectured about an issue or concern; it took an influential voice to expose, denounce, or reprimand evil, wrong, and mistreatment. Sojourner Truth demanded equal human rights for all women as well as for all African Americans through her speeches wherever she went. As often as she could, Eleanor Roosevelt advocated for expanded roles for women in the workplace, the civil rights of African Americans and Asian Americans, and the rights of World War II refugees. The Bible tells us that "a fool's mouth is his destruction....but the mouth of a righteous man is a well of life."

According to the Word of God, the tongue can speak life or death to the body, mind and soul. That is why as single people, we should be careful what we say. Even when people disrespect or misuse us, we must remember that the right words will turn away wrath. However, when we retaliate in an evil manner, only anger will surface. While this may appease our emotions instantaneously when we retaliate, it will grieve our soul and could possibly ruin our relationships. Since the tongue is a deadly tool innately, we need to monitor what we say and who we say it to. My Aunty El often gives me advice to let my words be few and full of grace. Although I occasionally find my words getting too lengthy and not as graceful, it is always my goal to resort back to her wise council. Whenever I follow that advice, I find my experiences are blessed and peaceful. This gives me to know that words can influence a situation, the mind, the body, and the spirit.

Single men and women should strive to be righteous, so that our words offer life to all we encounter. Why don't we decree for ourselves what we want to be and how we want to establish ourselves personally, spiritually, and socially. With the help of God, we as single women will order our tongue so that it is revived, corrected, and directed to give life and not bring death.

A Song to Sing:
If You Call on Jesus, He Will Answer Prayer

Verse 1:
If you call on Jesus (caller)
He will answer prayer (response).
(repeat)

Verse 2:
Call Him, Jesus, Jesus, Jesus (caller)
He will answer prayer (response)
(repeat)

Verse 3:
Call Mary's baby (caller)
He will answer prayer (response)
(repeat)

Verse 4:
Call the Lily of the Valley (caller)
He will answer prayer (response)
(repeat)

Verse 5:
Call the Bright and Morning Star (caller)
He will answer prayer (response)
(repeat)

(repeat as wanted and add verses to caller)

• • •

Order Your TONGUE

. . . .

Proverb 18:21
Death and life are in the power of the tongue: and they that love it
shall eat the fruit thereof.

Revelation 12:11a
And they overcame him by the blood of the Lamb, and by the
word of their testimony....

Oh, what a small, yet powerful tool! According to the word of
God, life and death are in the power of the tongue. When God
created the world, He spoke everything into existence. He
simply said, "Let there be..." and it appeared. On the other hand,
when Jesus was on earth, he gave us an example of speaking
death or curses. Jesus was hungry as He approached a fig tree.
However, when he arrived at the tree, the tree did not have any
fruit on it. Jesus cursed the tree by saying no fruit will grow on it
thereafter. When Jesus and the disciples passed by the tree the
next day, it had withered from the roots.

It's kind of like what I've heard others say..."What you say is what you get." If that is really so, then why do we make statements like the following? "You are killing me!" "I'm going to hurt you!" And how many parents correct their infants by saying "Bad baby!?" When my children misbehave, I do not call them bad. I call them active. When I'm not feeling well; rather than saying, "I'm sick." I say, "I have had better days." I refuse to declare sickness. I try not to associate negative words with my life. I try to carefully choose what I speak over my life and my family or call into existence. Likewise, we should be careful as to what we speak over our spouse or our marriage.

Someone once told me that the words we say are like little prayers. In other words, there is power in our words. The Bible even encourages us to speak those things that are not as if they were. If we only have faith, we can accomplish any and everything with the use of our tongue. Even Jesus said…if we have faith the size of a mustard seed (and do not doubt), we can speak to the mountain and tell it to jump into the sea…and it must obey.

So what if your words are like miniature prayers? What type of spouse are you praying for? What type of children are you claiming? In other words, what are you speaking into the life of your family? Are you calling them sorry, dumb, stupid, etc? Or are you calling them blessed and highly favored of the Lord? What are you speaking into your marriage? You see and know what you have or live with today; but what are you claiming for tomorrow? Regardless of how tough things are, are you declaring that things will get better for you? Are you speaking blessings of victory in Jesus over your life and/or marriage? With your mouth…speak it as you would have it to be. If it does not come suddenly, keep speaking it…until it comes to pass.

KEAISE & MONROE

According to Revelation, they overcame by the blood of the Lamb and by the word of their testimony. How we use our tongue determines whether we speak blessings or curses. What is the word of your testimony? Are you speaking victory or defeat? The choice is yours…and what you say with your tongue will ultimately be what you get. Life and death are in the power of the tongue. Once our words are out there, we cannot take them back (whether we mean them or not). Therefore, it is good practice to think twice before speaking once. Speak life into your family. Speak life and victory into your marriage.

A Prayer to Pray:

Heavenly Father,
As I open my mouth, speak through me. Help me to be very careful as to what I speak in and over my spouse, my marriage, my family, and even my life. Help me to speak blessings only. Help me to speak words of encouragement to build up and strengthen both my spouse and my family. In Jesus' name I pray. Amen.

• • •

Order Your
HANDS

· · · · · · · · · · · · · · · · · · ·

John 9:4
I must work the works of him that sent me, while it is day: the
night cometh, when no man can work.

Whatever you find your hands to do, you need to do it. This is
what I was taught from a child. Our hands are tools for God's
work, whether we are helping prepare a Sunday meal, cleaning
the church, or helping the elderly down the stairs. There should
never be a time when our hands are not doing good. As single
women our time is not obligated to a husband or family; we are
free to do as my Aunty El calls "God's work." This does not mean
our jobs are any easier, though. It can be quite the opposite.
God calls for willing workers, not lazy ones.

John 9:4 tells us that we should work while it is day, because
when the night comes we will not be able to work. As a brief
explanation of this scripture, I have quoted since a child, work
should be done when we have access, time, and opportunity.
This is comparable with working while it is day. When these
three things are no longer available, night comes and makes it

difficult to carry out our tasks. Night is equivalent to 1) when we get older, 2) when we are sick, or 3) when we lack opportunity. The single person's hands are equipped to serve, bring joy, and build lives; if it is done as unto God. While this sounds like a good plan of service, it requires hard work and constant encouragement to accomplish.

Ordering our hands means doing when we don't want to do; giving when we want to keep. Working to help our fellow man is rewarding naturally. When we work when it is not convenient or required, we serve God and man, which is spiritually rewarding. While some women are born with the gift of helps, single women should look for opportunities to use our hands whenever and wherever it's needed.

Two personal examples for me as a witness of such dutifulness came in the form of my two Aunts. My Aunts, Elflorence and Freddie Mae Oliver, allowed God to order their hands from childhood. No matter what the family needed, whether a meal prepared, a house cleaned, money loaned, clothes cleaned, hair groomed, or car washed; my two single aunts found a way to willing serve without pay. Now, the results of their examples have been passed on to their siblings and nieces in the form of us serving in our homes, community, churches, and workplaces. Somehow, my aunts' desire to please God and their love for family and friends exceeded laziness, financial increase, or self-centered ambition. What about us? If we want God to order our hands, we must be willing to go the extra mile by giving of ourselves to help those in need, encouraging those going through, cleaning the church when needed and taking time with young people who lack natural and spiritual guidance, to name a few.

A Song to Sing:
I Command My Hands to Serve the Lord

Verse 1
I command my hands to serve the Lord.
I command my hands to serve the Lord.
I command my hands to serve the Lord.
I command my hands to serve the Lord.
Hands serve the Lord
Hands serve the Lord.

Verse 2
I command my mouth to praise the Lord.
I command my mouth to praise the Lord.
I command my mouth to praise the Lord.
I command my mouth to praise the Lord.
Mouth praise the Lord
Mouth praise the Lord.

Verse 3
I command my ears to hear the Word.
I command my ears to hear the Word.
I command my ears to hear the Word.
I command my ears to hear the Word.
Ears hear the Word.
Ears hear the Word.

(Add verses as you are lead)

• • •

Order Your HANDS

Isaiah 59:1
Behold, the Lord's hand is not shortened, that it cannot save;
neither his ear heavy that it cannot hear...

1 Thessalonians 4: 11
And that ye study to be quiet, and to do your own business, and to
work with your own hands, as we commanded you...

When we think of our hands, we think about the tools we actually use to get things done. With our hands, we usually put into action the things we think about and/or talk about doing. How we choose to use our hands is totally up to us. God gives us a free will to choose to do good or to do evil in His sight.

Whatever we choose to do, we should do it sincerely before God and not unto man. We are encouraged by the Word to not let the left hand know what the right hand is doing. When we do our deeds, we don't have to sound a trumpet for the world to see and know what we are doing. God sees all that we do...and He will reward accordingly.

The Bible states that we will reap what we sow. Whatever type fruit we want to be produced in our life...is the kind of seed we must plant. On the other hand, if you don't want any fruit... don't plant any seeds. Beware though...the one who does not plant will not have anything to reap. Accordingly, if a man does not work, neither will he eat.

Paul encouraged the Thessalonians to quietly mind their own business and work with their own hands. In other words, do what you can to help yourself. I am a witness that when you honestly try to do the best you can, God will take care of that which you are not able to do. Even within marriages, God will take care of things. An individual cannot make his/her spouse do anything. However, one can live a Godly life before his/her spouse. We as Christians should be diligent in the things we do. Not only that, but we should always strive to do good so others, even our spouses, may see our good works and glorify God.

Also, we as children of God must remember...if or when we get off track and do things that are not in the will of God...God is there to help. Regardless of how far we allow ourselves to go, God's hand is not slack and it is not short. If He has to reach way down low, God is able and willing to lend a helping hand to mend, heal, and restore (even our marriages).

As God is so gracious and merciful unto us, we should be mindful to be gracious and merciful unto others (especially unto our spouses). We should diligently work while we have life within us. Also, whenever possible, we should readily lend a helping hand to others; especially to our spouses.

A Prayer to Pray:

Heavenly Father,
Please help me to diligently do good works with my hands. Help
me to sow good seeds in my marriage and family that we might
reap a good harvest. Let my deeds and actions bless both my
spouse and my family. In Jesus' name I pray. Amen.

• • • •

Order Your
FEET

· · · · · · · · · · · · · · · · · · · ·

Psalm 119: 105
Thy word is a lamp unto my feet, and a light unto my path.

Believe it or not, where we go will determine what we do. Every step we take as single women is important for our sustaining power and success. Since every good and perfect gift is from above, we can only expect good to come as we follow God's leading. If we would acknowledge God, He promised to order our steps. One of my favorite songs is *Order my steps in your Word Dear Lord; Lead me guide me every day; send your anointing Father I pray. Please order my steps in your Word.* This song is prophetic. Our feet should be ordered according to the Word of God. In the Book of Ruth, Naomi allowed God to order her steps despite pain, hunger, and embarrassment. Ruth allowed God to order her steps despite the possibility of never remarrying after the death of her husband. As a result, these single women found grace, power and success, because they submitted to God's leading.

What happens, though, when we don't allow God to order our

steps or follow His leading? I must use myself as the example here. From a child my Aunty El told me that God wanted me to be a servant. After asking her what kind of job would that be, she repeated herself and said, "God wants you to help those in need." This did not sit well of course with my ego; so I ventured to Claflin University with the thought of making lots of money but not with a spirit of servanthood. Since accountants are known for making substantial amounts of money and I made an A+ in my Accounting class during my senior year in high school, this seemed perfect for me. So I thought. As a single young woman, I ventured without God's leading into Accounting only to get a good paying job. The only thing was I didn't follow where God was leading. I followed my lust and desire.

Because my life was in God's hands, my plans failed and I ended up going in the direction God wanted me to go. Majoring in Business Administration with a minor in Marketing served well as a foundation to becoming a children's librarian. God has blessed me to serve children and the general public for over 20 years. My life shows the importance of letting God lead your life. As single men and women, we can save plenty of unnecessary steps by allowing God to order our feet.

A Song to Sing:
Let Jesus Lead You

Verse 1:
Let Jesus lead you, Let Jesus lead you.
Let Jesus lead you all the way.
All the way from earth to heaven.
Let Jesus lead you all the way.

Verse 2:
He's a mighty good leader, He's a mighty good leader.
He's a mighty good leader all the way.
All the way from earth to heaven.
Let Jesus lead you all the way.

Verse 3:
He led my mother, He led my father.
He led my sister all the way.
All the way from earth to heaven.
He led my brother all the way.

Let Jesus lead you, let Him lead you.
Let Him lead you all the way.
All the way from earth to heaven.
Let Him lead you all the way.

• • •

Order Your
FEET

. . . .

Romans 10:15
And how shall they preach, except they be sent? As it is written,
how beautiful are the feet of them that preach the gospel of peace,
and bring glad tidings of good things!

Ephesians 6:15
And your feet shod with the preparation of the gospel of peace;

When we think of our feet, we think of our God-given base for the body and our God-given mode of transportation. It is upon the feet that our body is able to stand tall. It is also with our feet that we are able to move the body from place to place. As we travel from place to place, we should be mindful of a few things. First, we should be mindful of where we are going. Next, we should be mindful of what we are carrying with us. Lastly, we should be mindful of the spirit in which we are moving.

As we travel and move through life, if we don't know where we are going...any road will get us there. We must live life with purpose and make sure the steps we take will get us closer to our desired destination. If by chance we realize we are headed in the wrong direction, we must quickly turn around and take steps to get us on the right track. Even with our marriages…if we suddenly realize that we have gotten off tract, we must be quick to pray, amend our ways, reconcile our differences, and get back on track.

Next, as we travel…we must always be mindful of the load that we are carrying. We can choose to be good news barriers or we can choose to be bad news carriers. As children of God, we should strive to be good news barriers. Even Paul said, "…how beautiful are the feet of them that preach the gospel of peace, and bring glad tidings of good things!" No, you don't have to be a preacher to share the gospel. As believers, we are commissioned in Matthew 28 to go spread the Good News. With the pressures and stress of life today, plenty of opportunities will exist to share the Good News…especially in the midst of challenging times. We must be mindful of the impact that things and other people have on our marriages.   As children of God, we must not allow any and everything to negatively impact our marriages. With some things and even with some people, we must let go and let God have his way.…

Not only should we carry glad tidings of good things, but we should also go in the spirit of peace. Yes, I realize that things can be hectic all around us. But as children of God, we should stand firm on the word of God and let the peace of God fill our hearts. Even in the midst of chaos and confusion, we should have feet that are swift to carry the Word of God in the spirit of peace. To whatever extent, by whatever means God has blessed us, we should be willing to go abroad, share the gospel, and be a blessing unto others (especially our spouses and families).

A Prayer to Pray:

Heavenly Father,
I ask You in the name of Jesus to guide my every step. Send me
Heavenly Father where You will have me to go. As I go, help me
to carry only what You desire me to carry with me or even bring
within my marriage and family. By all means God, help me to go
in the Spirit of Peace. In Jesus' name I pray. Amen.

• • • •

Order Your
MIND

. . . .

Isaiah 26:3
Thou wilt keep him in perfect peace whose mind is stayed on thee: because he trusted in thee.

There is a song that says, *"My hands belong to God; My feet belong to God; My mind belongs to God; My whole body belongs to God."* Yes, we do belong to God. But are we at peace with God? In order for us to reap the benefits of being at peace with God and our fellow man, we must allow God to be the focus of our minds. The Bible assures us that God will keep us in perfect peace if our minds are stayed on Him. For a long time this was not very clear to me, because I thought it meant thinking about God all the time. As time went on and life's experiences took their courses, it became clear that my mind should always be about God's will and purpose for my life—not my own agenda.

So many single men and women have in mind what we want to be, who we want to associate with and how we want to live. That's normal. While this is important when setting life's goals, this should not be the driving force behind our motives. Yes, we should plan how we want to live, who we should associate with and what we want to be; but we should make sure it is within God's will for our lives. Our minds belong to God! Because He made us and know who we are, we should depend on Him to keep our thoughts pure. The growth that we acquire depends on the way that we order our minds. This is no small feat. It is a gradual development that gets better with practice.

As single men and women, it is so easy to get distracted with associations. The saying, "Great minds think alike" has some truth to it. If we think like God, we will be great like Him. Great minds enjoy collaborating; hence, we don't need to associate with people who are living below our spiritual standards. Having a sound mind will cause us to have selective and productive relationships. God is our present help and will lead, guide and protect us when we put our minds on His will and His purpose for our lives. Then our associations will be beneficial to our growth spiritually, financially, and socially.

We will not look at what we have, who we know, and where we are going to give us peace. God is the only one that can bring peace to our minds when we order it in His will.

A Song to Sing:
Mind of Christ My Savior

Verse 1;
May the mind of Christ, my Savior, Live in me from day to day,
By His love and pow'r controlling
All I do and say.

Verse 2:
May the Word of God dwell richly
In my heart from hour to hour, So that all may see I triumph
Only through His pow'r.

Verse 3:
May the peace of God my Father
Rule my life in everything, That I may be calm to comfort
Sick and sorrowing.

Verse 4:
May the love of Jesus fill me
As the waters fill the sea; Him exalting, self abasing,
This is victory.

Verse 5:
May I run the race before me, Strong and brave to face the foe,
Looking only unto Jesus
As I onward go.

Verse 6:
May His beauty rest upon me, As I seek the lost to win,
And may they forget the channel,
Seeing only Him.

• • •

Order Your
MIND

· · · · · · · · · · · · · · · · · · · ·

Isaiah 26:3
Thou wilt keep him in perfect peace, whose mind is stayed on thee:
because he trusteth in thee.

Philippians 4:8
...whatsoever things are of good report; if there be any virtue, and
if there be any praise, think on these things.

The mind is a very powerful tool. It is so powerful that the rest
of the body functions according to what's taking place in it. In
my opinion, the mind is kind of the powerhouse or the control
center of the body. Even if the rest of the body is in perfect
condition, if the mind is not functioning properly...it throws the
whole body off.

A lot of things start and stop right there in the mind. If a person
thinks he/she can do something, chances are they can and will
do it. However, if the same person thinks in his/her mind that
a task is too difficult and impossible for him/her to perform,
there's a good chance that the outcome will line up with the

mind...and he/she won't do it. Even the Word of God tells us...as a man thinketh in his heart so is he.... So what do you think of yourself? If you think you are a success...a success you are. If you think you are a failure...a failure you are. What do you think of your marriage?

Since the mind is so powerful and influential in the way our lives are lived, it is vitally important that we protect the contents of the mind. As thoughts and ideas come to mind that are not for our good or to the glory of God, we must quickly replace those thoughts and ideas. If we are going to flourish and stay afloat in this world, we must keep our minds filled with things that inspire and uplift us. As negative thoughts come to mind, we must replace them with positive thoughts. As we magnify the Lord in our mind...we will see problems begin to minimize in our mind and world.

Paul says, "if there be any virtue, if there be any praise, think on the good things." That's exactly what we have to do. Life will be filled with some good and some bad times. Marriage will be filled with some good and some bad times. Once something has happened, we cannot change it...even if we want to. However, what we can change or control is our response to the things that happen in our lives. Rather than dwelling on the negatives, we can focus and think on the good. We can choose to think on the negative and become depressed and down-trodden...or we can think on the good and be uplifted and encouraged to keep on keeping on.

Remember, it is in the mind where a lot of things start. If we truly want to overcome and make it in this world, we must keep our minds stayed on the Lord and let the mind of Christ be in us.

Some things we cannot handle on our own. If we let them, the things of the world will overwhelm us. But as we keep our minds on Christ and let the Word of God and the Spirit of Christ take residence in our hearts, nothing shall over-power us. Because of our faith and trust in the Lord, God will keep us in perfect peace. Regardless of what comes up against us or our marriages, we can survive. With the help of the Lord and the mind of Christ dwelling in us, we can handle it; we can take it; and we shall make it!

A Prayer to Pray:

Heavenly Father,
Help me to keep my mind stayed on You and not the things of the world. Even in my marriage, help me to not dwell on the negative, but fill my mind with the good things and the good times of my marriage. In Jesus' name I pray. Amen.

• • • •

Order Your
HEART

· · · · · · · · · · · · · · · · · · · ·

Jeremiah 17: 9 - 10
The heart is deceitful above all things, and desperately wicked: who can know it? I the Lord search the heart, I try the reins, even to give every man according to his ways, and according to the fruit of his doings.

According to the Bible, we are born in sin and shaped in iniquity. Since we know that the heart is desperately wicked, it would behoove us to pray for God to clean our hearts daily. The heart can be changed when we ask God to change it and we are willing to make that positive change.

Change came when Rahab, the prostitute in the Old Testament, wanted to change her heart. When given the opportunity to change, Rahab accepted the true and living God by protecting God's chosen men from their enemy. This single woman, Rahab, risked lying to the king of Jericho to hide and allow the Israelite spies to escape. Because of her willingness to help God's people, she saved herself and her family.

Rahab's change of heart put her in the position to get a blessing from God. What about when we desire wrong things and do things that are displeasing to God. Like Rahab, we too, can accept God's invitation of salvation by first believing that God can make us better. No doubt Rahab felt unworthy, insufficient, and unclean because of her lifestyle. Yet, she believed that God could change her if she took the first step toward changing her heart.

It is important to note that blessings from God come in more than just riches. In Rahab's case, she received a tender heart toward God. This caused her to do the right thing. Not only were their lives spared naturally, they were saved and given eternal life spiritually; thus, our prayer as single women should be for God to change our hearts every day. Even in the little things like being nice to those who are rude, giving to those we feel don't deserve it, or helping those who misuse and abuse us, one can show change of heart.

As single men and women, we have the power to change our future if we change our heart toward God. This change includes releasing our deceitful, wicked, hateful, and evil hearts. When we make that change, God can and will do great things in our natural and spiritual lives. Let's make our goal today that we will order our hearts to serve God.

A Song to Sing:
Change My Heart Oh God

Change my heart oh God, Make it ever true.
Change my heart oh God, May I be like you.

You are the potter, I am the clay.
Mold me and make me, this is what I pray.

(repeat as wanted)

• • •

Order Your
HEART

. . . .

Matthew 12:34-37
O generation of vipers, how can ye, being evil, speak good things?
For out of the abundance of the heart the mouth speaketh. A
good man out of the good treasure of the heart bringeth forth
good things: and an evil man out of the evil treasure bringeth forth
evil things. But I say unto you, that every idle word that men shall
speak, they shall give account thereof in the Day of Judgment. For
by thy words thou shalt be justified, and by thy words thou shalt
be condemned.

The heart is the nucleus of the body. It is the life of things. When
the heart stops beating, life as we know it ends. So it is with
relationships; especially marriages. When the heart is no longer
in it, the relationship draws to an end. For that reason, married
people must guard their hearts and be careful not to let their
love for their spouses wax cold.

Every day will not be a happy day (a ray of sunshine). You will
have some rainy days that are very challenging. Every word may
not be kind. Every word may not be a word of encouragement.

WOMEN OF ORDER: **ORDER IN THE BODY**

However, regardless of how our spouses treat us, we must respond with love and respect. If not for the love and respect of the spouse, we must do it out of love, respect, and obedience to God.

As a married individual, you cannot make your spouse love you. Neither can your spouse stop you from loving him/her. Regardless of whether you are loved or despised; praised or preyed upon; lifted up or put down by your spouse, you must keep a loving heart. After all, you are not responsible for what your spouse does or says to you. Your spouse is responsible for his/her actions and must give an account to God accordingly. However, you must one day give an account for how you respond to what your spouse does or says to you. By all means, let your response and words be kind and sweet because one day you might have to eat them.

Whether you are treasured or treated like trash, you should act like a jewel (or pearl). If you struggle with doing so, just consider yourself as a diamond in the rough. By all means though, keep a loving heart and you will one day come forth as pure gold.

As married individuals, we must guard our hearts. We must be careful not to let our hearts become bitter when things do not go as we desire. Regardless of the ups and downs of a marriage, we must keep our hearts pure before God. We must keep our hearts filled with love in and through it all. We must love until death does the separating. God will work things out for us in His own time in His own way.

A Prayer to Pray:

Heavenly Father,
Please guide me and keep my heart filled with love. If there are any ill feelings in my heart for my spouse, my family, or anyone else, please remove them. Let the love of Christ fill my heart and replace any and all manner of darkness. Fill my heart with good things that I may produce good fruit. In Jesus' name I pray. Amen.

• • • •

Conclusion

As we go forth in life, we must strive to honor the order God has ordained. When we do things God's way, God will give us favor and always honor His Word. In a world where there seems to be no stability, God's Word is true, firm, and sure. His Word will never fail. We can always count on it and trust it in the midst of any and all circumstances, as we pray and praise our way through.

The single perspective was ended with a song of encouragement; while the married was ended with a prayer. The two symbolize the midnight experience of Paul and Silas. When they were in jail, at midnight, Paul and Silas prayed and sang praises unto God. As they worshipped God through songs and prayers, their chains were loosed and the doors of the prison were opened. Perhaps it is midnight in your life or in your marriage. As Psalms 67 reveals, when praises go up, blessings come down. At our darkest hour, we must constantly read God's Word and faithfully worship Him through songs and prayers; then we must trust God and watch Him break the chains that have our lives or relationships (whether married or single) in bondage. Although midnight experiences will come, Ms. Shiela and I realize that if we keep God first and order our lives (especially our relationships) according to the will of God, brighter days will come.

About the Author
SHIELA M. KEAISE

· · · · · · · · · · · · · · · · · · · ·

I have known Shiela M. Keaise for many years now. I have heard her speak at church functions and I have carried my children to her Story Hour at the local library. I have also had the privilege of working directly with Miss Shiela on several projects at the library. It was with a video project that I had the opportunity to observe Miss Shiela's work ethnics.

Miss Shiela is a very enthusiastic person. She is very creative and passionate about her work. When she makes up her mind to do something, she gets it done (with or without the cooperation of others). I have found Miss Shiela to be very easy to work with. She welcomes suggestions and ideas from others. Not only does she ask for it, but when she receives feedback, she utilizes it.

Miss Shiela is very patient and enjoys working with others, especially children. She seems to look for opportunities to use and develop the skills of others. If others want to be included, she will find a way to get them involved. I have come to realize that one of her greatest love is singing. She involves singing in just about everything she does. It is her true comfort zone. She sings on her job. She sings for fun, and she sings for the Lord.

Miss Shiela's greatest attribute is that she is a God-fearing woman. As ideas come to her, she prays and seeks the will of God for her life. She has very strong spiritual convictions and as she feels led of God, she is willing to follow. I, personally, am honored to have had Miss Shiela to ask me to work with her on this project. I pray that God will use our efforts to bless many.

*– **Magdline Monroe***

• • •

About the Author
MAGDLINE MONROE

. . . .

Besides being the wife of a gospel preacher, Magdline Monroe is the mother of seven gifted children. She is a mentor to many women and respected by all who know her. Mrs. Monroe has been married for 25 years to Rev. Mark T. Monroe and enjoys sharing her insight of wisdom and knowledge as God leads.

She proved that education is important and obtainable by graduating Valedictorian of her class at the McCrorey-Liston High School (of Blair) and Summa Cum Laude at Voorhees College, both in South Carolina. Mrs. Monroe received her Mathematics degree and worked for a while before becoming a full-time house wife and mother. After her youngest child started school, Mrs. Monroe went on to receive a Masters in Education from Columbia College (also in South Carolina).

The way Mrs. Monroe protects her children prove that she is a mother of passion and compassion and qualifies as a pattern for women everywhere. Not only has Mrs. Monroe shown professionalism in videography, she is a trainer, an organizer, a youth leader, Sunday school teacher, math teacher, and

57

motivational speaker.

Her minor in computer science opened the door to the congenial working relationship she and I have developed over the years. This mother, wife, mentor, and author is effective in whatever her hands find to do, because she practices what she teaches. After knowing Mrs. Monroe for over ten years, it is easy to identify her as an effective communicator, a caring concerned mother, and a first-class example for married women. God never errors when he calls us for a mission.

– Shiela M. Keaise

• • • •

Upcoming book in the Women of Order series:

Order on the Job

Both authors will offer advice, experience, and God's word to encourage women on how to have order on the job.

If you have any questions or issues you want us to address, please email us:
TheDreamMotivators@yahoo.com